Origins

Downhill Racers

Alex Lane and Tom Worsley
Character illustrations by Jon Stuart

Contents

OXFORD
UNIVERSITY PRESS

Feel the speed

If you think skateboarding is all about jumping kerbs and sliding down ramps, then think again!

There is a type of skateboarding where riders zoom down a hill at speeds of over 100 kilometres per hour (kph). It's called downhill skateboarding – and it's fast and furious!

This is the rider Martin Siegrist. You can find out more about him on page 24.

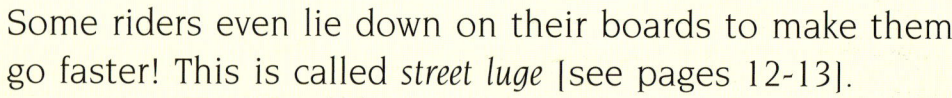

Some riders even lie down on their boards to make them go faster! This is called *street luge* [see pages 12-13].

Downhill skateboarding is a 'gravity sport'. This means that the riders move by using the power of gravity – the force that pulls objects downwards. The longer and steeper the road or track, the faster the board moves.

Gravity

Try rolling a ball down different slopes. Which is faster?

Imagine going that fast on a skateboard!

This is the rider Jonathan Martinez. He lives in the Alps in France, so he can get lots of practice on the long, steep hills.

Downhill skateboarding

Downhill skateboarding is also known as 'stand-up' or 'speedboard'. Riders use specially designed skateboards that allow them to travel down hills at very high speeds. The boards are designed to go faster than normal skateboards.

Riders can reach speeds of up to 112 kph!

This is Douglas Silve. He is bent forwards in a *tuck* position (see pages 10-11).

112 kilometres per hour! I wouldn't want to go that fast!

A downhill skateboard

All skateboards have three main parts: the deck, wheels and trucks.

1 **Deck**: this is the long flat board that the rider stands on. The top surface is often **concave** so that it is easier for the rider to grip and turn the board with their feet.

2 **Wheels**: downhill skateboards have 4 wheels. They are bigger than normal skateboard wheels. Big wheels will roll faster than small wheels, and they are also better at going over bumps in the road.

3 **Trucks**: downhill boards have 2 trucks. These are the metal **axles** that provide steering and join the wheels to the board.

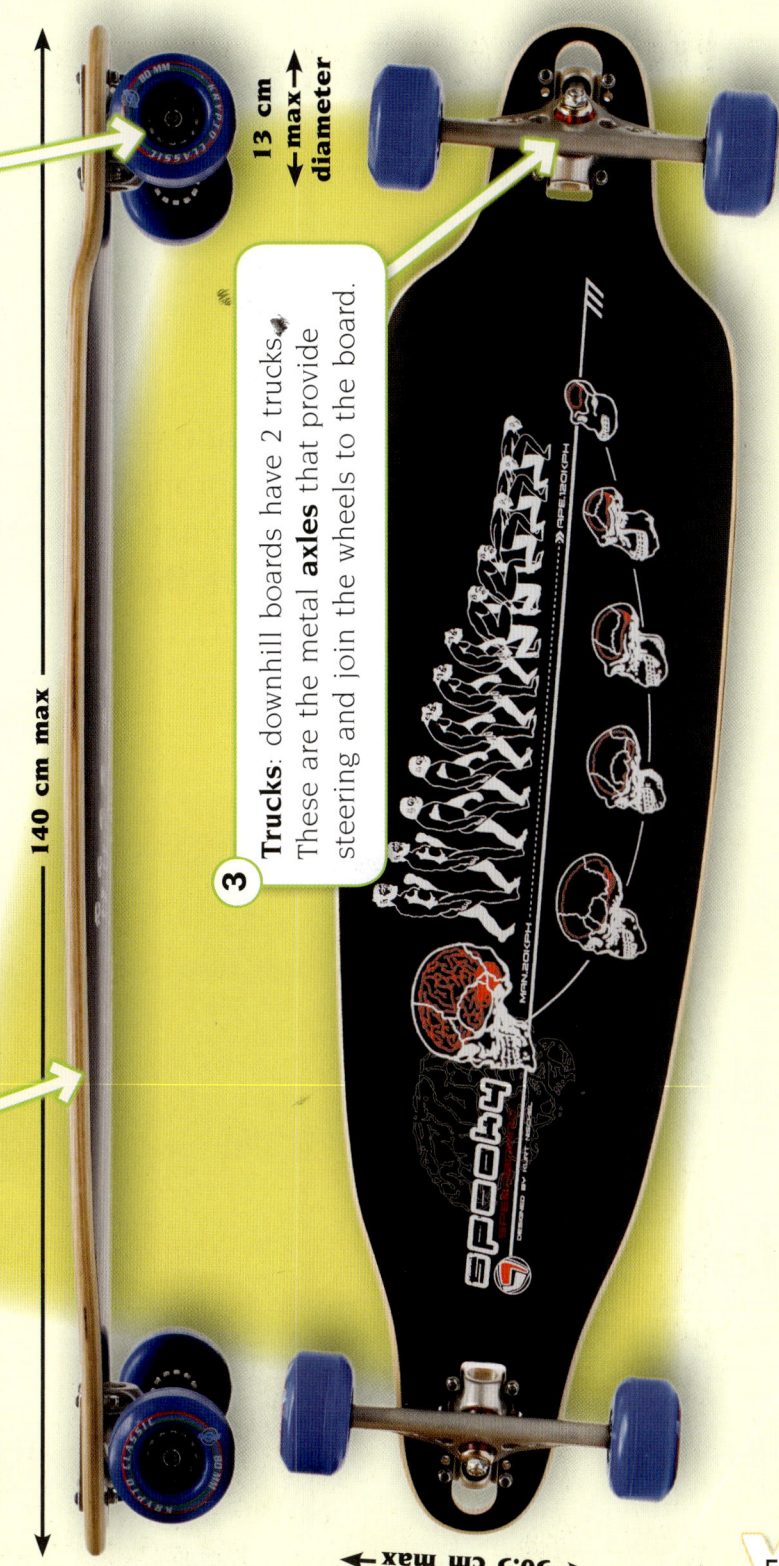

13 cm
← max →
diameter

140 cm max

←— 30.5 cm max —→

Rider safety

It is very important for riders to think about safety.
This means:
- their own safety
- safety of other riders
- safety of **spectators**.

Downhill and street luge are not sports that you
can do at home, without any proper training or
safety equipment. Each rider must look after
their own safety and make sure their equipment
is safe to use in a competition.

Stephen Daddow crashes into
the barrier at Mount Panorama,
Bathurst, Australia, March 2008.

Before a race, riders must have their safety equipment inspected. Each rider must wear:

1

Helmet: a hard shell helmet is essential. It must have full-face protection and the strap must be done up tightly.

2

Leather suit: all riders wear a special leather suit. Leather is tough and thick. It helps to protect the rider from cuts or grazes.

3

Gloves: riders wear special, thick gloves with plastic plates on the palms. Riders have to put their hands on the road when they are cornering to stop them tipping over. The plastic plates allow them to do this without hurting their hands.

4

Footwear: skateboard shoes should be comfortable with flat bottoms. They must be in good condition and be fastened tightly.

5

Back protector: downhill riders must wear a special armoured back protector to prevent any injuries to their back or spine.

SAFETY FIRST! DOWNHILL SKATEBOARDING IS EXTREMELY FAST AND DANGEROUS AND SHOULD NOT BE TRIED AT HOME.

Getting started ... by learning to stop!

Downhill skateboards do not have any brakes! So it is very important to be able to stop safely. All riders need to learn how to footbrake. This starts at home, not on a hill.

1 First you must find a smooth, flat surface to practise on. Then you need to practise dropping your foot on and off the board. This gets you used to the feel of contact between your foot and the ground.

2 Next, you should try the braking action. Keeping your weight over your 'standing' foot, gently lower the braking foot on to the floor. The braking foot should slightly roll from the heel to the ball of the foot, with your toes curled upwards inside your shoe. You must practise this at a walking pace to start with.

The most important thing is not to try and stop yet! It is important to brake gently. If you brake too hard, you will fly off. So you must try and slow down your speed, then put your foot back on to the board and continue to roll along.

3 When you are comfortable slowing down, you can try braking harder so you stop. You must not practise this on a hill until you have learnt to do it at home.

If you drag the sole of your shoe along the road at 100 kph, it will quickly burn a hole in your shoe. So downhill racers will often glue a piece of rubber to their shoes to make them last longer.

I wonder how long my shoes would last?

Sometimes riders will brake so hard that clouds of smoke will come off the sole of their shoe! This is because of the heat caused by **friction** between the bottom of the shoe and the road surface.

Going fast

Air **resistance** is the force between air and another material. The more air resistance, the less easily something will move through the air.

Some shapes, called *streamline* shapes, cause less air resistance than others. They are often smaller at the front so they 'cut' through the air. Think about the shape of an aeroplane. They are designed to be streamlined so they move through the air easily.

A person standing upright creates lots of air resistance because the air has to pass up and over the person.

Downhill skateboarders lean forwards and put their arms behind their back to make themselves look as small as possible from the front. This body shape is called a *tuck*.

This way, the rider is more streamlined so they will move through the air more easily. They meet less air resistance than a rider standing upright on a board.

When a rider lies down on a board, they make themselves even more streamlined and meet even less air resistance. This is why a street luge rider will often be able to go faster than a downhill rider.

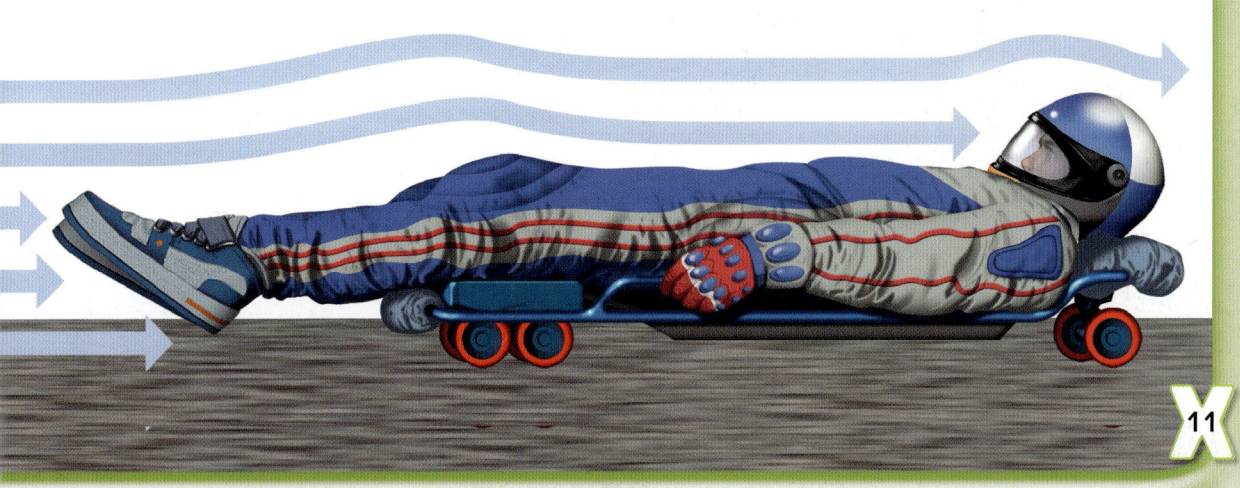

Street luge

Street luge was invented by downhill skateboarders who wanted to go even faster! Special boards were made. They had more wheels so they could grip the road better. They also had handles for the rider to hold on to, and a headrest at the back. Street luges look more like sledges than skateboards. They can travel at speeds of up to 135 kph!

A rider's head is only about 15 cm from the road. From this level, you can see your chest and your feet. You can see things flying past you, but you can't see round the next corner or over the next bump. Riders have to use their **instinct** when riding street luge. They also have to make sure they know the course well before they start.

To steer round bends, riders have to move their bodyweight. They do this by sitting up or leaning. To brake, the rider will drag their feet on the ground (see pages 8-9).

You'd have to be really brave to do that!

A street luge

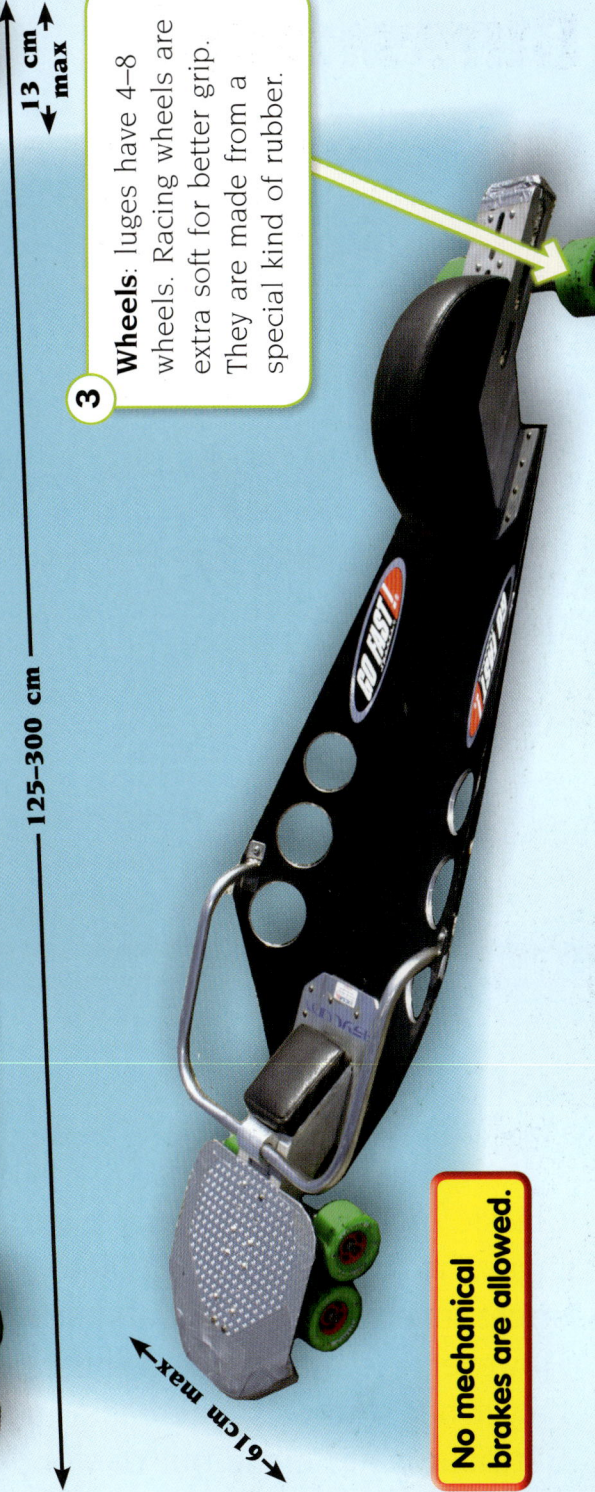

1 **Chassis**: the chassis must be **structurally** sound. It must not have any sharp edges which could injure riders. All boards must pass a technical inspection before a rider can race. Luges must pass a *stress* or *bounce* test to prove they are safe.

2 **Trucks**: luges have 2–4 trucks. They are a lot wider than standard skateboard trucks. The rider steers by leaning from side to side.

3 **Wheels**: luges have 4–8 wheels. Racing wheels are extra soft for better grip. They are made from a special kind of rubber.

13 cm max

125–300 cm

◄61cm max.►

No mechanical brakes are allowed.

Classic luge

Riley Meehan (USA) footbrakes on his classic luge before entering a corner in Jungholtz, Austria at Almabtrieb 2007.

Classic luge, also known as 'buttboard', **preceded** street luge. The first races took place in 1975 in California. As with street luge, buttboard riders sit or lie down on their boards. However, the boards are a different shape. A buttboard is flat. It has 4 wheels whereas a luge can have up to 8 wheels. Buttboards are made out of wood whereas luges are made out of metal and other materials.

A buttboard

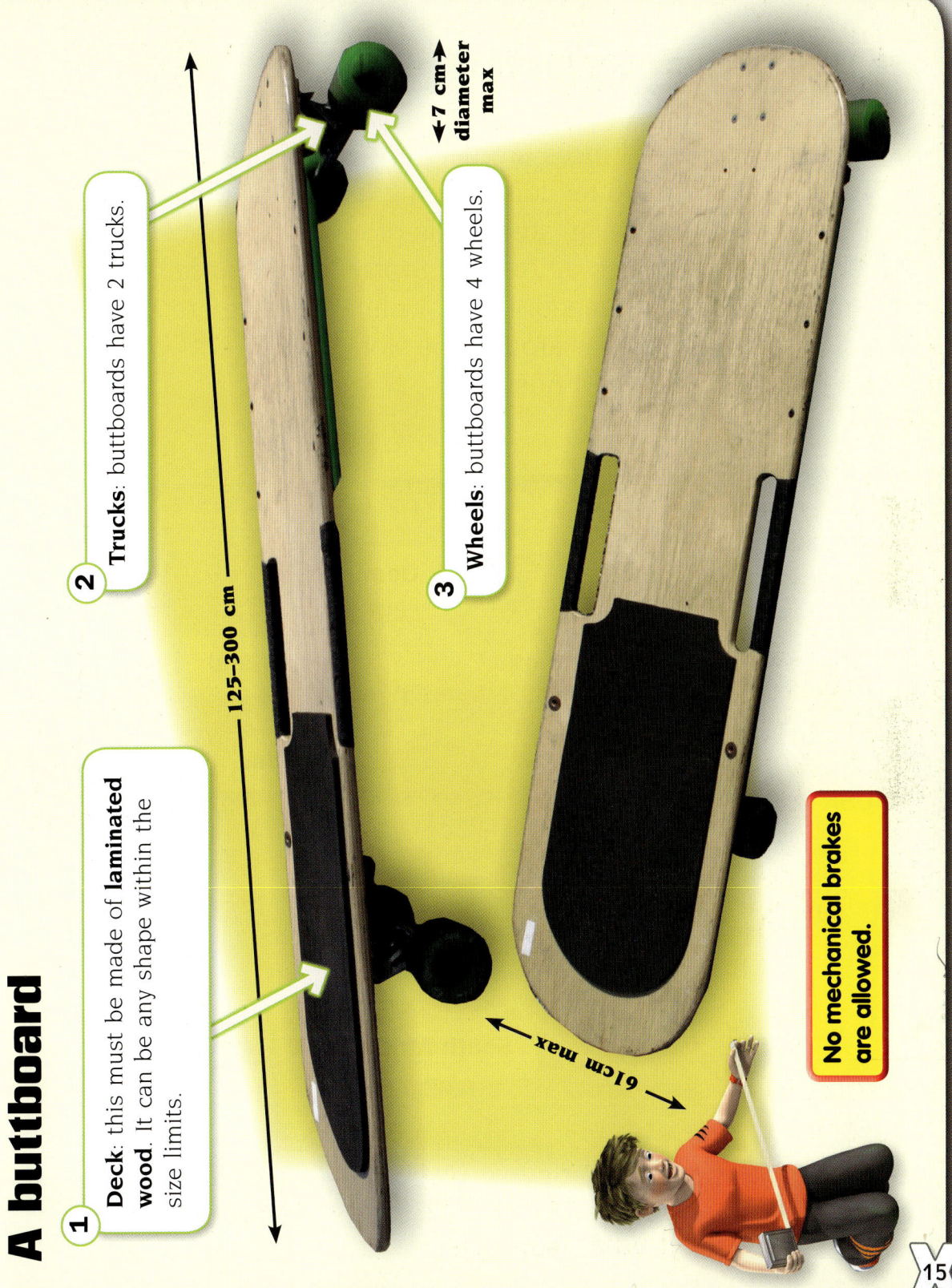

1 **Deck**: this must be made of **laminated wood**. It can be any shape within the size limits.

125–300 cm

2 **Trucks**: buttboards have 2 trucks.

←7 cm→ diameter max

3 **Wheels**: buttboards have 4 wheels.

61cm max

No mechanical brakes are allowed.

15

Courses and tracks

Downhill skateboard races are held on roads between two and three kilometres long. Racing is most popular in places that have long, steep hills or mountain roads – countries such as Austria, Switzerland, France, Germany, USA and Canada. But downhill and luge are becoming more popular around the world, in the UK and in South Africa and Australia.

Canada

UK

Germany

Switzerland

France

Austria

USA

South Africa

Australia

Downhill hotspots.

marshal

straw bales

These riders are keeping well away from the edge! This is just one of the many corners of the Maryhill Loops Road, USA.

Races are only held on closed roads (roads that are closed to traffic). There are safety marshals, and an ambulance crew on standby in case of a crash.

These roads are specially chosen because they need to be smooth, steep, and with sharp corners. This makes the race interesting for the riders as well as all the **spectators**.

If there are any dangers, such as trees or rocks along the side of the road, then the race organizers will build walls of straw bales around the dangerous things. Then, if the riders have a crash they will crash into the straw instead of hurting themselves. As much as 50 tonnes of straw can be used to make a race course safe.

Here are three of the world's most famous downhill race courses. What can you see? What things do they have in common?

Maryhill (USA)

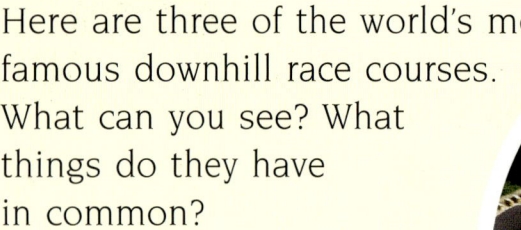

Bathurst (Australia)

These look like tough courses.

Eastbourne (UK)

Racing lines

Riders are at their fastest when they are going in a straight line. Therefore, the fastest way round a corner is by the straightest route. This may not be the shortest route. The lines that riders take when they are racing are called *racing lines*.

Most mistakes are made at corners. Riders are competing for the same racing lines. Sometimes they may have to take a slower route so they don't crash. If you can corner well, you are more likely to win the race.

Slow

Fast

Here, two riders are competing for the same racing line round a corner.

The Races

Like many sports, riders have to **qualify** in order to take part in a proper race. Competitors are allowed at least two practise runs before making a qualifying attempt. But they only get one chance to qualify. There are several different types of races:

1. **Time trial:** a single rider races against the clock. After lots of riders have raced, the person with the quickest time wins!

2. **Dual:** two riders race against each other.

3. **Mass:** four riders compete against each other. The first two riders go through to the next round.

4. **Super mass:** up to six riders race against each other. The first three riders go through to the next round.

5. **GP format:** GP stands for Grand Prix (which means 'Big Prize' in French). It is based on the format used in Formula 1 car racing. The rider with the fastest qualifying time starts at the front and the slowest starts at the back. A maximum of 24 competitors are allowed to enter.

Riders ready!

The World Cup

Every year, a series of races is held all over the world. This is called the *Downhill Skateboarding World Cup*.

The winner of each race gets points. You can also earn points for coming second, third or fourth. There are often as many as two hundred riders at each event, so the competition is fierce.

At the end of each World Cup year, all the points are added up. Whoever has won the most points is declared the World Cup Champion.

These are the winners of the Downhill World Cup race in Eastbourne in 2008.
- 1st Scoot Smith (Canada)
- 2nd Pete Connolly (United Kingdom)
- 3rd Christopher Sanne (Norway).

Each competition can last from three to five days, depending on how many people enter. There is no limit on the number of riders who can take part. It takes a long time to get through all the qualifying heats, so the riders have to be very patient to wait their turn.

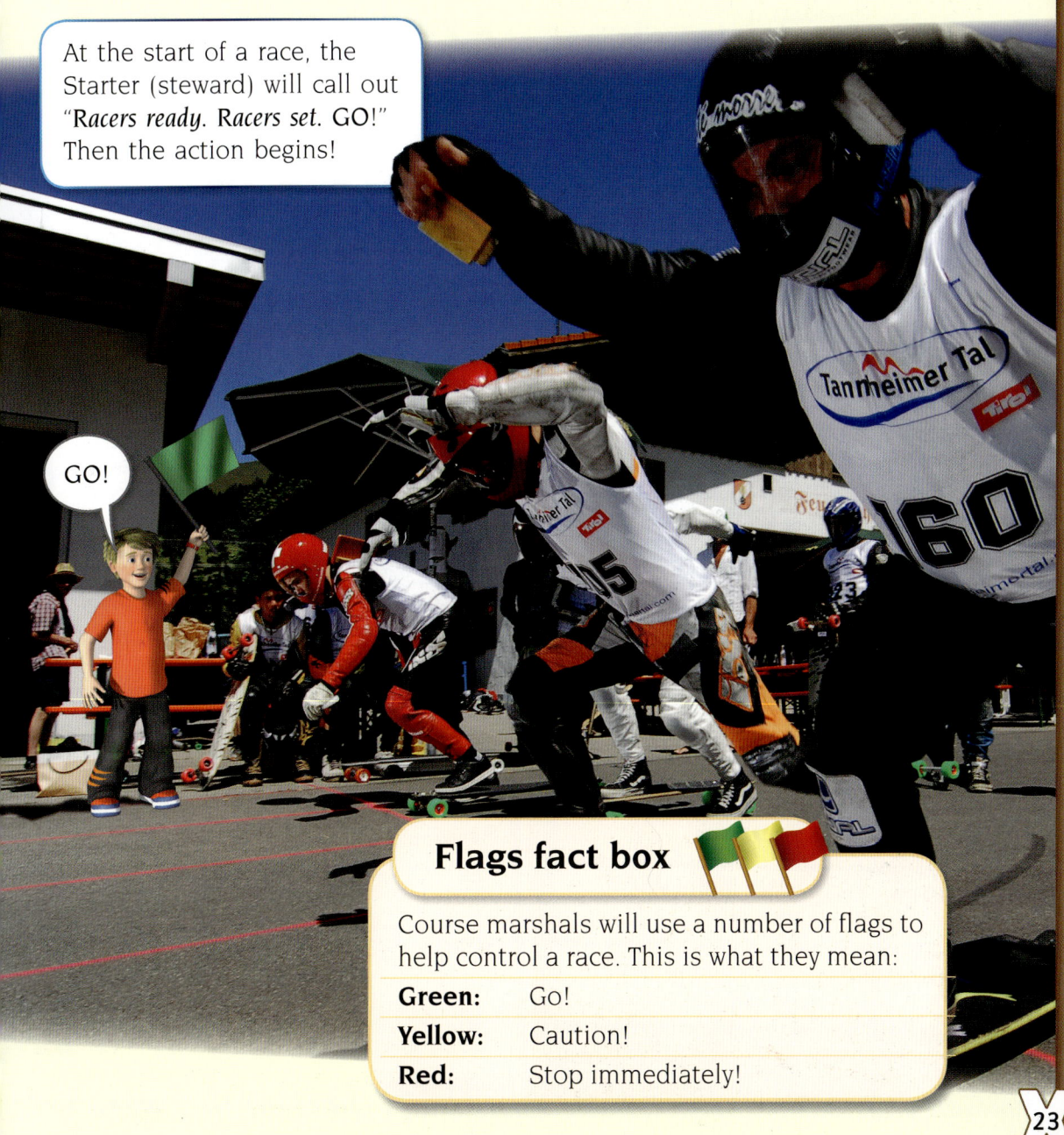

At the start of a race, the Starter (steward) will call out *"Racers ready. Racers set. GO!"* Then the action begins!

GO!

Flags fact box

Course marshals will use a number of flags to help control a race. This is what they mean:

Green:	Go!
Yellow:	Caution!
Red:	Stop immediately!

Meet the Riders!

RIDER PROFILE

Name:	Martin Siegrist
Nickname:	Sigi or Robot
Date of birth:	19/11/1980
Height:	172 cm
Weight:	63 kg
Country of birth:	Switzerland
Skating for:	since he was a child (why walk when you can skate?), racing since the 1990s
Event:	Downhill
Ranking:	13th in the World, 2007
Achievements:	World Champion 3 times

RIDER PROFILE

Name:	Pete Connolly
Nickname:	Long Board Pete/ Dark Knight
Date of birth:	01/09/1978
Height:	193 cm
Weight:	82.5 kg
Country of birth:	England, St. Albans.
Skating for:	since 1999
Event:	downhill
Ranking:	8th in the World 2007, No. 1 in the UK
Achievements:	5th in Australia World Cup race, 2008, 2nd at Eastbourne, 2008

RIDER PROFILE

Name:	**Stephen Daddow**
Nickname:	**Bear**
Date of birth:	**19/06/1971**
Height:	**175 cm**
Weight:	**75 kg**
Country of birth:	**Papua New Guinea**
Skating for:	**since 1981**
Event:	**downhill and slalom**
Ranking:	**10th in the World, 2007**
Achievements:	**World No. 3 in 2003, made front cover of *Concrete Wave* magazine**

RIDER PROFILE

Name:	**Jackson Shapiera**
Nickname:	**Jacko**
Date of birth:	**23/03/1989**
Height:	**183 cm**
Weight:	**70 kg**
Country of birth:	**Australia**
Skating for:	**longboarding since 2002, slalom racing since 2007, downhill since 2008**
Event:	**downhill and slalom**
Ranking:	**7th in the World, 2007**
Achievements:	**2nd at Rock and Roll, Austria**

RIDER PROFILE

Name:	Joel King
Nickname:	Joel (Gravity) King
Date of birth:	28/01/1980
Height:	170 cm
Weight:	79 kg
Country of birth:	Tanzania
Skating for:	since 2002. Competed in first World Cup in 2003.
Event:	street luge and classic luge
Ranking:	18th in the World, 2007. No. 3 UK, 2007
Achievements:	UK National Street luge Champion, 2006. Guinness World Record holder on a powered street luge

RIDER PROFILE

Name:	Mike River
Nickname:	River
Date of birth:	4/10/79
Weight:	63.5 kg
Country of birth:	UK
Skating for:	since 2005, downhill since 2008
Event:	downhill
Ranking:	30th in the World, No. 2 in UK 2007
Achievements:	not crashing in the Euro Races!

RIDER PROFILE

Name:	Chiara Poscente
Nickname:	Ra
Date of birth:	19/05/1984
Height:	173 cm
Weight:	68 kg
Country of birth:	Alberta, Canada
Skating for:	skating/racing since 2006
Event:	downhill
Ranking:	3rd in the World, 2007
Achievements:	holds the unofficial women's speed record at over 115 kph

RIDER PROFILE

Name:	Rebekka Gemperle
Date of birth:	18/10/1984
Height:	176 cm
Weight:	62 kg
Country of birth:	Switzerland
Skating for:	since 2007
Event:	downhill
Ranking:	4th in the World
Achievements:	2nd at Eastborne World Cup, 2007

Rider interview: Tom Worsley

Tom Worsley is Chairman of UKGSA (United Kingdom Gravity Sports Association). He travels all over the world racing, in between doing his day job. He even has a growing fan club (although he is a bit embarrassed by this). Find out more about why he does what he does, and how he got started.

Tiger: How long have you been skateboarding for?

Tom: *I got my first skateboard when I was five. I started doing street luge and downhill in 1999. I did my first World Cup race in 2001 in Aviemore in Scotland.*

Tiger: Where did you come?

Tom: *I came ninth – but mainly because there weren't many other riders there! There were only about twenty or thirty riders there but none of the world's best.*

Tiger: How did you start?

Tom: *A friend of mine first got me started. He introduced me to street luge. I had no idea what I was letting myself in for!*

Tiger: Where and how did you learn?

Tom: *I learnt to ride at a course in Salisbury. Other riders taught me. That's the way it works. It's one of the reasons I started the UKGSA – to give people the chance to train safely on closed roads. People contact me via my website and we offer lessons and training. I've taught a lot of riders who are now much quicker than me!*

Tiger: Do you need to be a skateboarder?

Tom: *Not especially with street luge. You just need to be brave! Pretty much anyone can pick it up with the right training and if they have the right equipment.*

Tiger: Why do you do it?

Tom: *Not many companies make skateboards specifically for downhill or street luge. Many riders make their own equipment. That appealed to me. I am an engineer. I liked the idea of building a board. I wanted to find that secret that would give me the advantage over another competitor. Over the years I have made about twenty boards. The other reason I do it is for the sheer excitement!*

This is Tom on his luge.

Tiger: Do you get scared?

Tom: *I've been scared. I was scared after I injured myself. Before you seriously hurt yourself, you think you are invincible. The fear comes later. Once, I was practising on a road in North Wales. We had an official road closure so there were no cars allowed on it, but the road was wet and dirty. At the bottom of the road was a sharp left turn followed by a bridge and a stone wall, then a cattle grid. I hit the bridge and broke my ankle and my foot. It really hurt! It changed my outlook. I missed a whole season of riding. I also had to have six months off work. After that, I found it difficult to get back on the luge board again – even on a track that I was used to. It was fear. It was something I had not experienced before that point.*

This is an X-ray of a broken ankle joint. This is what Tom did. It is a reminder of how dangerous this sport can be – even for a top rider.

That looks painful!

Tiger: But you didn't give up completely?

Tom: *No, I still wanted the feeling of going fast. That is when I started doing stand up (downhill). It was not an easy change to make. The techniques are different. The lines you take on the road are different. It was difficult at first and I got lots of bruises. Then someone helped me and showed me what to do. They taught me how to slow down and brake.*

Now I ride both downhill and street luge. Most people only ride one of these. I'm one of only two or three riders in the world who do both.

Tiger: How much of your time does this take up?

Tom: *Organizing the world championships is like a full time job. It takes up a lot of my free time. I have to fit that in with my day job.*

Tom in his helmet.

Glossary

axle	a rod passing through the centre of a wheel or group of wheels
chassis	the base frame of a vehicle with wheels
concave	a shape that curves inwards
diameter	the distance across a circle, through the centre
friction	one surface rubbing against another
grid	a pattern of lines that mark the starting places on a racing track
instinct	something that makes people and animals do things they have not learnt to do – they can just do them
laminated wood	thin layers of wood glued together to make a wooden board
mechanical	done or made by machinery
precede	to come before something
qualify	to get enough points to go on to the next part of a competition
resistance	to fight against something
spectator	someone who goes to watch an event
structural	relating to a part of a stucture

Find out more about gravity sports

The International Downhill Federation:
http://www.internationaldownhillfederation.org

UK Gravity Sports Association:
http://www.ukgsa.org